Mission: ME

An Interactive Bible Study to draw closer to Christ.

By Kimyetta E. Hayden

ISBN: 9781731357984

DEDICATION

This book is dedicated to my loving husband, Vilroy and my inspiring children, David, Mark and Hannah. You are my personal mission that God placed in my lap before the beginning of time. I'm honored to walk in my greatest calling in life…as a wife and a mother.

This book is also dedicated to the precious women of New Hope Baptist Church in Fayetteville, Georgia. You are the inspiration for this study. Your tears, your laughter, your heartache, your questions, your answers, your faithfulness, and your determination provided the foundation for this study. Thank you for the privilege and honor to serve you in Life Groups. Thank you for providing the canvas for the Lord to paint upon my heart in the pages of this book. You are indeed my Jesus Sisters!

TABLE OF CONTENTS

Introduction: Messed up too?

Let's Begin!

Week 1: Are you thirsty?

Week 2: Are you consistent?

Week 3: Are you letting God in?

Week 4: Are your desires changing?

Week 5: Let's Review

Week 6: Are you making the Bible real?

Week 7: Are you walking with God and not in front of Him?

Week 8: Are you giving up?

Week 9: Let's Review

Week 10: Are you loving people, even if you don't like them?

Week 11: Are you under pressure?

Week 12 Are you...?

To obtain the Mission ME small group leader outline, visit

KimyettaHayden.com.

Matthew 5:6

Blessed are those who hunger and thirst for righteousness, for they will be filled.

Introduction

Messed up, too?

It was October 1, 1999 and I sat anxiously in a jam-packed room of women at Times Square Church in the heart of New York City. I was sitting in a room of women that varied in age, racial background, ethnic makeup, and socioeconomic status. I didn't know anyone in the room and yet I felt comfortable, but still *slightly* anxious.

I didn't know any scriptures or worship songs. I didn't know much about the Christian faith. It was the first video Bible study I had ever attended. Who knew such a thing existed as a video Bible study anyway? What I knew is that as a new believer in Jesus Christ, all I wanted was this "new" Jesus that had infiltrated my life. So, there I sat in this Friday night Bible study in the middle of Times Square at the age of 25. When the Bible study started, the facilitator began to speak. Honestly, I don't remember much about what she said. However, when she turned on the video, my life would never be the same.

Music began to play on the video and then a thin, excited, blonde woman appeared on the screen. She began to speak about freedom. She spoke fast at times and slower at other times. She shared her testimony of how God walked her out of bondage into the marvelous light. Her passion and zeal for the Lord were infectious. I had never heard the term "stronghold" before. But on that day, I knew I had a kindred spirit with this sister on the video. I was thrilled to know there was at least one more human being on the face of the earth that had "things" in her head like me.

As I sat there, in the packed room, tears began to roll down my eyes uncontrollably. There were tears of pain of years of suppressing and hiding my personal "strongholds" and there were tears of joy because finally I heard someone share what I had experienced for a long time. I even laughed as I thought: *Wow, this lady was really messed up, just like me!*

That woman was Beth Moore, who later became the world-renowned Bible teacher that helped ignite the current, popular video Bible study movement today. On that night, I wrote in my notes, *I can do this. I should host a women's Bible study group.* Did I mention I was only 25? Since that day I have attended countless video Bible studies and my life has changed tremendously. I'm married with three beautiful children and I currently facilitate ladies Bible studies regularly.

This Bible study, **Mission ME**, is a collaborative effort that started 20 years ago in that room in New York City and continues today as I have the honor of serving women in my home church. I've had the privilege of facilitating ladies Bible studies for the last few years. I've cried with women, laughed with women, prayed with women, and walked with women as they endeavor to grow in their relationship with Christ.

Throughout the years, I've seen women face quite a few personal issues. Sadly, these issues are what consistently keep us in strongholds and under pressure. They also keep us from growing in our walk with Christ. **Mission ME** is more than just a weekly Bible study. This book is interactive. So much so, that it will challenge you to take up a new "mission" each week.

In the *Mission Impossible* movies, the protagonist must complete "missions" in order to save the universe from ultimate destruction. We won't have to complete missions to save the universe, but as we complete our weekly missions, we will have a chance to save our future, save our walks with Christ, and perhaps even make a lasting mark on our children and grandchildren. I can assure you, this journey won't be easy because let's face it: life is hard. **However, when our desire to change outgrows our desire for personal comfort, then perhaps we will push past our feelings to complete what we start.**

We will draw upon Psalm 63:1-8 as a foundation to seek the heart of Christ. **Our ultimate objective is to draw closer to Jesus Christ each day...and desire more of Him than the day before.** Romans 12:2 says we will be transformed by the renewal of our minds. Not only will we endeavor to transform our minds, but we will seek to develop spiritual disciplines that will help shape our hearts as well.

So, your mission, should you choose to accept it, is on the next page. If you turn the page, you are accepting the challenge to become a better version of you...it's the you God intended you to be when He created you.

Will you join me?

Isaiah 43:19

Behold, I am doing a new thing; now it springs forth, do you not perceive it? I will make a way in the wilderness and rivers in the desert.

Let's Begin

Before any mission begins, it's important to understand where you are. Can you imagine starting a new job without knowing where to find your desk or workspace? If you didn't know where to start, then you could aimlessly walk the halls for eight hours before going home. That's why it's important to understand where to start... *your start.* Every start is different. Some women are new in the faith, while others have been studying God's Word for many years. Regardless of where you are in your walk with Christ, everyone has a starting place.

On a scale of 1-5 (1 being poor and 5 being outstanding), how would you rate your current spiritual temperature? (**NOTE**: *Spiritual temperature is a phrase to describe how close you sense God in your everyday life. Does He seem close and intimate or does He seem distant?*)

_____

Why did you choose the above?

_____

_____

_____

_____

_____

_____

On a scale of 1-5, how would you rate your <u>desire</u> to grow closer to Jesus Christ?

_____

Why?

_____

_____

_____

_____

_____

_____

_____

_____

_____

In your opinion, what are three things holding you back from having a more fulfilling relationship with Christ?

_____

_____

_____

_____

_____

_____

_____

_____

_____

_____

_____

Read the NIV or NASB version of Psalm 145:18.

What's the hardest part about the reality of this scripture?

_____

_____

_____

_____

_____

_____

_____

_____

_____

_____

Each week (or two) we will focus on one theme designed to help you become more reflective and proactive in your walk with Christ. At the end of each devotional passage, you will answer a few short questions before reading **"Your Mission"**. Upon completing your mission, check off the boxes and record your thoughts for the week and prepare to discuss in your group sessions. *(Note: Its okay if you're reading the book alone.)*

WEEK 1
ARE YOU THIRSTY?

Psalm 63:1
You, God, are my God, earnestly I seek you; I thirst for you,
my whole being longs for you, in a dry and parched
landwhere there is no water.

I have a book on my shelf written by a fantastic Christian author entitled *Thirsty*. I purchased the book many years ago because I love the title and the author, so I knew it would be a great read. (Also, it was only $1 for a hard cover at a library sale.) The challenge is that I was indeed thirsty. However, I wasn't willing to do much about it outside of the normal Christian stuff, like going to church and quick devotions, etc. I wasn't willing to stretch myself beyond the norms.

It took many years of angst and pain before I really made a definitive decision to do something about my thirst. Did you notice I used the word *definitive*? Definitive is another way of saying final, complete, end of the road, that's it. You see, as a Christian, I was thirsty, but I wasn't disciplined. I wanted more of God in my life, but I wasn't willing to give up certain things that kept me away from Him. I was parched to the spiritual core but lacking the focus to reach for Him.

Does my story sound familiar? God designed us in such a way that we would experience thirst and He would always be the one to fill it. No amount of sex, alcohol, gossip, shopping, social media, friends, spouses, kids, careers, church and money can fill the thirst that's already in us. He created us, so wouldn't He know how to fill us? The question is whether we're thirsty enough to pursue Him more than anything else in our lives.

Consider what the Psalmist wrote in Psalm 63. NOTE: Please read this VERY SLOWLY and THINK ABOUT THE WORDS.

"O God, you are my God; earnestly I seek you; my soul thirsts for you; my flesh faints for you, as in a dry and weary land where there is no water. So, I have looked upon you in the sanctuary, beholding your power and glory. Because your steadfast love is better than life, my lips will praise you. So, I will bless you as long as I live; in your name I will lift up my hands. My soul will be satisfied as with fat and rich food, and my mouth will praise you with joyful lips, when I remember you upon my bed, and meditate on you in the watches of the night for you have been my help, and in the shadow of your wings I will sing for joy. My soul clings to you; your right hand upholds me." (ESV)

The Psalmist was thirsty, but He did something about it. According to verses 3-8, he did a number of things to quench his thirsty soul. In fact, by the time he got to verse eight, he's "clinging" to God. Wow, I simply love that picture of me clinging to God, so let's make this a week where we commit to fulfill our thirst by clinging to Him and holding on for dear life!

Your scripture: Please write Psalm 63:1 in the space below:

_____

_____

_____

_____

_____

_____

_____

_____

Your scripture: In the NIV Bible, the Psalmist uses the word "earnest." Look up the definition of earnest and write what it means on the lines below.

_____

_____

_____

_____

_____

_____

Are you "earnestly" seeking God daily? Why or Why not?

_____

_____

_____

_____

_____

_____

How does the Psalmist practice inspire you in your walk with Christ?

_____

_____

_____

_____

_____

_____

_____

_____

_____

_____

Your Mission:

Find a place in your home and commit that space to become your "prayer closet." Spend at least 7 minutes a day **praying out loud** and talking to God in your new prayer closet for at least five days. Start out the week by asking God to help you cling to Him and allow Him to fill your thirsty soul. *(Disclaimer: your prayer "closet" doesn't have to be a physical closet. It can be a chair in your home or sitting in your car before you leave for work each day or sitting in your bathtub.)*

❏ **Mission Complete-** Day 1 - Find a Prayer Closet/ Pray for seven minutes
❏ **Mission Complete-** Day 2- Pray for seven minutes
❏ **Mission Complete-** Day 3- Pray for seven minutes
❏ **Mission Complete-** Day 4- Pray for seven minutes
❏ **Mission Complete-** Day 5- Pray for seven minutes

❏ **All Missions Completion Date:**

_____

Mission Notes:

_____

_____

_____

_____

_____

_____

_____

Your journal: Record your thoughts for the week. Any victories or defeat?

_____

_____

_____

_____

_____

_____

_____

_____

_____

_____

_____

_____

_____

_____

_____

GROUP SHARE
After Week 1

WEEK 2
ARE YOU CONSISTENT?

Hebrews 12:11
No discipline seems pleasant at the time, but painful. Later
on, however, it produces a harvest of righteousness and
peace for those who have been trained by it.

There's one thing I know for certain about consistency: *I
have been consistently inconsistent throughout my life.* When
I think about the enormous amount of responsibilities I have
as a wife, mother, teacher, business owner, life coach, and
author, I feel completely inadequate. Sometimes, my
thoughts of inadequacy caused me to shrink back from what I
needed to do and simply put my head under a pillow, instead
of staying focused on establishing consistency in different
areas of my life.

It took many years before I understood what the writer of
Hebrews meant in chapter 12 verse 11 by stating "No
discipline seems pleasant at the time, but painful. Later on,
however, it produces a harvest of righteousness and peace for
those who have been trained by it." Imagine that: God knew
that being consistent and disciplined would hurt. In fact, He
uses the word "painful." However, I rejoice when I read the
second part of the scripture that says it produces a harvest!
Hallelujah! I can shout over that because I know how to push
forward and discipline my flesh to be consistent because
He's already informed me that there's a reward at the end.
I can be consistent in my eating habits because the harvest is
a healthier, leaner body with a smaller waist line. I can be
consistent in my personal Bible study because I'll reap a
harvest of increased knowledge of Christ. I can be consistent
in my prayer life because I know I'll reap a harvest of greater
intimacy with Christ.

Remember Hebrews 12:11 the next time you're dreading the treadmill or some other aspect of your life that requires discipline. It'll be worth it. Don't allow the lack of personal discipline to keep you from spending time with God each day. You never know the reward He has waiting for you that can only be reaped in His Holy presence.

Your scripture: Please write Psalm 63:2 in the space below:

_____

_____

_____

_____

_____

_____

_____

Your scripture: What do you think the Psalmist meant in Psalm 63:2 when he said, "I have looked upon you in the sanctuary?":

_____

_____

_____

_____

_____

_____

_____

_____

_____

_____

_____

_____

How can you get the help you need for consistency by considering the Psalmist phrase "I have looked upon you in the sanctuary?" *(Also, read Psalm 121:1-4 for a hint.)*

_____

_____

_____

_____

_____

_____

_____

_____

_____

_____

_____

_____

_____

_____

_____

_____

Your Mission:

In the lines below, write one area in your life that requires you to be consistent TODAY. After which commit that area to God in prayer and ask Him to help you establish the proper discipline in your life to become more consistent. Follow through for the next five days by praying over this mission.

_____

_____

_____

_____

_____

_____

_____

_____

❑ **Mission Complete** - Day 1 - Identify one area in your life that requires more consistency and pray about it.

❑ **Mission Complete**- Day 2- Pray about consistency in that area for at least seven minutes.

❑ **Mission Complete**- Day 3- Pray about consistency in that area for at least seven minutes.

❑ **Mission Complete**- Day 4- Pray about consistency in that area for at least seven minutes.

❑ **Mission Complete**- Day 5- Pray about consistency in that area for at least seven minutes.

❑ **All Missions Completion Date:**

_____

Mission Notes:

_____

_____

_____

_____

Your journal: Record your thoughts for the week. Any victories or defeats? Do you have any personal revelation?

GROUP SHARE
After Week 2

WEEK 3
ARE YOU LETTING GOD IN?

*But seek ye first the kingdom of God, and his righteousness;
and all these things shall be added unto you.*
Matthew 6:33 (KJV)

On the surface, one would think this topic of "letting God in" should be first and foremost. However, it is intentionally in week three for a reason. Oftentimes in our walk with Christ we think we're letting God guide us. We fool ourselves into believing God is first because we may pray every morning, or we may ask God for guidance on an issue. However, letting God into your life is so much more. When Jesus said 'seek ye first the kingdom of God and his righteousness and everything will be added unto you,' (Matthew 6:33), I don't think He meant it in a literal sense *alone*. The Hebrew word for seek is chaqar, which means to search for, search out, examine or investigate. Another meaning translates 'to spy out'.

Are we truly seeking God by examining, investigating and spying out His character and His will? During our devotion time, are we getting before Him like a private investigator earnestly seeking to know more about Him? Do we examine and re-examine His Word in order to fully understand His heart?

Sisters, that's what I believe 'letting God in' is all about. When our life's mission involves an earnest, continuous pursuit of Jesus, not His stuff, but simply Jesus, then we can comfortably walk in the knowledge that He permeates our every being and then He can add everything unto us. So, let's be intentional about truly letting Him in this week.

Your scripture: Please write Psalm 63:1-3 in the space below (all three verses). Use a yellow or pink highlighter to highlight every verb. *(Note: A verb is an action word, such as seek, run, clap, etc.)*

_____

_____

_____

_____

_____

_____

_____

_____

_____

_____

_____

_____

_____

_____

_____

_____

Your Mission:

Think of yourselves as a private investigator on a mission to track down and learn more about this Jesus. Create your own character profile by reading any sections from the synoptic gospels (Matthew, Mark, Luke or John). Write seven-character traits that you uncover about Jesus. By the end of the week, pray over the traits and thank God for being ever present in your life and invite Him in to take over.

Jesus is:

TRAIT	SCRIPTURE REFERENCE
Example: Compassionate	*Matthew 9:36*
1.	
2.	
3.	
4.	
5.	
6.	
7.	

❑ **Mission Complete- Day 1** - Identify seven-character traits of Jesus and write above.
❑ **Mission Complete- Day 2**- Pray about the seven-character traits.
❑ **Mission Complete- Day 3**- Pray and invite God in to transform you more into the image of Christ.
❑ **Mission Complete- Day 4**- Repeat from the previous days.
❑ **Mission Complete- Day 5**- Repeat from the previous days.

❑ **All Missions Completion Date:**

_____

Mission Notes:

_____

_____

_____

_____

_____

_____

_____

_____

_____

Your journal: Record your thoughts for the week. Any victories or defeats? Do you have any personal revelation?

GROUP SHARE
After Week 3

WEEK 4
ARE YOUR DESIRES CHANGING?

Psalms 37:4
Delight thyself also in the Lord: and he shall give thee the
desires of thine heart. (KJV)

Writing this week's study is a confirmation upon a confirmation for me. For the past week, the above scripture has been before my eyes in various ways. When I opened my devotional, I read it. When I turned on the television, I saw it. This morning, without knowing I would address this topic today, I spent a great amount of time, praying over this scripture. The whole notion of personal desires is HUGE for me. I wrote HUGE in all caps because God delivered me from some pretty powerful strongholds that lasted more than three decades and my deliverance all began when I cried out to God with the simple phrase: LORD, PLEASE CHANGE MY DESIRES. HELP ME TO WANT WHAT YOU WANT FOR ME.

I learned that phrase many years ago. I wish I could say that my desires changed instantly. It took many years of me praying that prayer and then backing it up with my actions. I couldn't ask God to change my desire for certain movies and television shows and then turn around and watch them. It took years for me to surrender to God's plan and will. I prayed that prayer and then began disciplining my flesh slowly, one day at a time before He completely changed my desires in certain areas.

This week's scripture is so important because oftentimes we want God to give us the desires of our heart without us delighting ourselves in Him. We want to eat ice cream every day without picking up the calories. We want beautiful skin and hair without drinking water and we want to be in great physical shape without doing any exercise. Looking back, if God had given me the desires of my heart in my sin sickened state, then I would've ruined my marriage and my family. I would be an insufferable cad of a person without any friends, any direction and any Jesus- *for sure.*

The beauty of knowing Jesus intimately is that as you spend quality time with Him each day, then your desires begin to align themselves with His desires for you. Are you willing to submit your personal desires to Him today?

Your scripture: Please write Psalm 63:4 in the space below:

_____

_____

_____

_____

_____

_____

_____

_____

_____

Your scripture: Thinking about Psalm 63:4, how can changing our desires, "bless the Lord" in our lives?

_____

_____

_____

_____

_____

_____

_____

_____

_____

Your Mission:

Be honest. Name one desire in your life that's keeping you from experiencing true freedom and fellowship with Jesus. Take it to Him in prayer this week and ask Him to change your desires, one day at a time.

_____

_____

_____

_____

_____

_____

_____

_____

_____

❑ **Mission Complete- Day 1** - Identify one desire you want God to help you change.

❑ **Mission Complete- Day 2-** Pray about your desires every day.

❑ **Mission Complete- Day 3-** In prayer, ask God to sanctify your desires.

❑ **Mission Complete- Day 4-** In prayer, ask God to make your desires Holy.

❑ **Mission Complete- Day 5-** In prayer, ask God to give you the desires of your heart.

❑ **All Missions Completion Date:**

_____

Mission Notes:

_____

_____

_____

_____

_____

_____

_____

Your journal: Record your thoughts for the week. Any victories or defeats? Do you have any personal revelation?

_____

_____

_____

_____

_____

_____

_____

_____

_____

_____

_____

GROUP SHARE
After Week 4

Ezekiel 36:26

And I will give you a new heart, and a new spirit I will put within you. And I will remove the heart of stone from your flesh and give you a heart of flesh.

LET'S REVIEW.

Review is a formal assessment with the possibility or intention of instituting **change** if necessary.
(Google definition)

Week 5: Review

I have an advantage.

I have the advantage of writing this book after facilitating quite a few ladies Bible Study groups. One of the greatest challenges that women face in Bible Study is the speed at which we move. Oftentimes we go from week to week of studying new material. The material is great and helpful for women. And yet, women still struggle with changing.

As a result of this observation, I have incorporated several sessions dedicated to reviewing, recapping, and renewing our commitment to what we have learned. Perhaps, it's the teacher in me. I learned many years ago the phrase "repetition is the mother of all learning." I can certainly attest to that, because some of the most lasting change I've ever experienced came from me watching or listening and studying the same material over and over again. Most people believe 21 days of change creates a new habit. However, in recent weeks I have studied more about the brain and learned according to Dr. Caroline Leaf that it actually takes 63 days to create new habits. That's what we want. We want new habits which will create greater spiritual disciplines, and ultimately, deeper intimacy with Christ.

What was the theme for week 1? *(Hint: The themes are at the top of each new week number.)*

_____

_____

What was the theme for week 2?

_____

_____

_____

What was the theme for week 3?

_____

_____

What was the theme for week 4?

_____

_____

Based on the first four weeks, which week was most impactful to you?

_____

Why?

_____

_____

_____

_____

_____

_____

Based on the first four weeks, which week was the most challenging to do?

_____

Why?

_____

_____

_____

_____

_____

_____

_____

_____

After the first four weeks, share what you are doing differently in your personal relationship with Christ? If you haven't changed much, what can you do differently for the next four weeks? (Feel free to go back through the previous missions.)

_____

_____

_____

_____

_____

_____

_____

_____

GROUP SHARE
After Week 5

WEEK 6
ARE YOU MAKING THE BIBLE REAL?

I have hidden your word in my heart, that I might not sin against you. Psalm 119:11

Before I read my Bible I ask God to make the words on the page come alive in me as I'm reading. I ask God to illuminate the words in such a way that I hear and understand *something* from Him. I started doing this because I used to read the entire Bible every year, while following one of the online Bible reading plans. I followed the yearly reading plan and simply read every day and then congratulated myself for my accomplishment in December because I checked off Bible reading every day of the year.

The challenge was that I was reading the Bible in order to check it off my "to do" list. I wasn't reading it to change my life. I wasn't reading the Bible as a living, breathing, viable being that I needed in my life every day. Therefore, I had to rethink my approach to the Bible. I started looking at the Bible as a necessity instead of a recreational luxury. I wanted God to make it come alive in me by hiding the words in my heart, like the Psalmist stated. 'I have written your word in my heart, so that I might not sin against you (Psalm 119:11). This was huge for me.

Nowadays, I don't simply read the Bible, I allow the Bible to read me. I take the words in the Bible and meditate on them over and over. If I'm struggling in an area, then I don't just read whatever comes next in my Bible. I take time to find scripture that relates to my situation and I read it over and over and then write it down and then I carry it with me and memorize it and get it inside of me in order to transform my thinking, which ultimately has transformed my life. I promise you: if you allow the Word of God to drip into the recesses of your heart, you will experience significant change.

Your scripture: Please write Psalm 63:5 in the space below:

_____

_____

_____

_____

_____

_____

_____

Your scripture: In verse 5 of the NIV Bible, the Psalmist compares his satisfaction in God with the fatness of food. Think about your last trip to a restaurant (especially a buffet). Did you feel so full that you couldn't imagine taking another bite of food? When was it and with whom?

_____

_____

_____

_____

_____

_____

_____

Think about the feeling of physical fullness from eating and reflect on whether you've ever felt so full and satisfied in God's Word? When did you feel full and satisfied? (Personal Example: Whenever I listen to Andy Stanley's series entitled, Free, I feel full and overflowing with excitement. Another example is when I recite 15 or 20 scriptures out loud during my prayer time, I feel full because God's Word is flowing freely through me during prayer.) What is your example? (DISCLAIMER: If you don't have one yet, then it's okay.)

_____

_____

_____

_____

_____

_____

_____

_____

_____

_____

_____

Your Mission:

Find one scripture that corresponds to an area in your life that you need to address and spend this week memorizing and meditating upon that one scripture.

❏ **Mission Complete- Day 1** -Identify one challenging issue in your life and pray.

❏ **Mission Complete- Day 2**- Find one scripture that corresponds to that area.

❏ **Mission Complete- Day 3**- Start memorizing the scripture.

❏ **Mission Complete- Day 4**- Work on memorizing the scripture.

❏ **Mission Complete- Day 5**- Work on memorizing the scripture.

❏ **All Missions Completion Date:**

_____

Mission Notes:

_____

_____

_____

_____

_____

_____

_____

Your journal: Record your thoughts for the week. Any victories or defeat?

_____

_____

_____

_____

_____

_____

_____

_____

_____

_____

_____

GROUP SHARE
After Week 6

WEEK 7

ARE YOU WALKING *WITH* GOD AND NOT IN FRONT OF HIM?

I will instruct you and teach you in the way you should go;
I will counsel you with my loving eye on you.
Psalm 32:8

Do you map out plans without consulting God? Do you initiate your "good" ideas instead of His ideas for you? Do you plan things based on what you've always done at church, work, or at home?

I did.

I'm considered the Lucille Ball in my home because I often come up with different "things" for our family. The challenge with my "things" is that I used to do so many "things" that were never apart of God's will for me. In fact, I'd often end up in a conundrum and then wonder, "where's God?"

Of course, God always rescued me out of my latest, greatest miscue. However, at a certain point it occurred to me that I should no longer walk out in front of God and then pray for Him to come and help me. I changed my prayers to humble myself to God's plan. One of my favorite scriptures says, "I will instruct you and teach you in the way you should go, and I will guide you with my eye." (Psalm 32:8)

Think about it. The awesome God of heaven and earth WILL instruct me and show me what to do and where to go and how to live. I don't have to come up with my grand plans. I simply have to seek Him, so He can instruct me. I trust His plans and His will so much more than my own.

Your scripture: Please write Psalm 63:6 in the space below:

_____

_____

_____

_____

_____

_____

_____

Your scripture: In the NIV Bible, the Psalmist "remembers" God upon his bed. The Greek transliteration for "remember" is mnaomai, which means "to be mindful." How does being mindful connect to walking behind God and not in front of Him?

_____

_____

_____

_____

_____

_____

_____

Your Mission:

Identify one area (or project) in your life that you concocted on your own and honestly lay it down before God. Spend the week asking God to instruct you and teach you where to go and what to do and then wait patiently for Him to do so.

❑ **Mission Complete- Day 1** -Identify one area you need to lay before God.

❑ **Mission Complete- Day 2**- Pray about it using the guideline in Your Mission.

❑ **Mission Complete- Day 3**- Pray about it using the guideline in Your Mission.

❑ **Mission Complete- Day 4**- Pray about it using the guideline in Your Mission.

❑ **Mission Complete- Day 5**- Pray about it using the guideline in Your Mission.

❑ **All Missions Completion Date:**

_____

Mission Notes:

_____

_____

_____

_____

_____

_____

Your journal: Record your thoughts for the week. Any victories or defeat?

_____

_____

_____

_____

_____

_____

_____

_____

_____

_____

_____

_____

_____

_____

_____

_____

GROUP SHARE
After Week 7

WEEK 8
ARE YOU GIVING UP?

Psalm 27:13-14

I remain confident of this; I will see the goodness of the Lord in the land of the living. Wait on the Lord; be strong and take heart and wait for the Lord.

Have you ever felt like giving up? I mean, not giving up on something easy like a diet plan. I've done that a lot over the years. I mean, have you felt like giving up on you... giving up on the fight to finish well. I remember struggling so terribly in my addictive thought patterns one day, that I felt my heart long to just quit and forget about Christianity all together.

There I said it... I actually entertained thoughts to simply leave behind the life I knew as a believer. Besides, non-Christians *appeared* to get all the breaks and have all the fun. When my husband was laid off his job in 2008, we struggled to eat and feed our children. But then I'd see unbelievers making money and taking vacations. I struggled to make friends while, my non-Christian neighbors threw big parties and barbecues all summer. I struggled to go to work to an oppressive job, while my unbelieving friends appeared to be fulfilled and happy on their jobs.

I was discouraged. So yes, I felt like giving up.
But then, the thought occurred to me... if I give up, then what?

What happens after I say goodbye to whatever I'm quitting on-? It could be a marriage, a diet plan, a tough relationship, a job... what next? What happens after you throw in the towel on the Bible Study or the "lazy" husband? What's on the other side of it?

You never know what's on the other side of the pain after you've completed the process.

The point for this week is to NEVER GIVE UP... The psalmist said I am certain that I will see the LORD's goodness in the land of the living. Wait for the LORD; be strong and courageous. Wait for the LORD. (HCSB)

If you're in the midst of a challenging situation, seek God and ask Him to give you a heart to press on, my sister.

Your scripture: Please write Psalm 63:7 in the space below. This time, please use the version from either NIV, KJV or ESV.

_____

_____

_____

_____

_____

Your scripture: In verse 7, there's a word that begins with the letter "h" in the verse. Write that word in the space below.

_____

In your own words, how would you define this word?

_____

_____

_____

_____

_____

Turn to Psalm 121:1-8 again. Read all eight verses slowly.

_____

Your Mission:

Please go to your web browser (that's the place where you look up web sites on the internet.) Go to Google. Type in "Psalm 121 + The Brooklyn Tabernacle Choir." Listen to the choir sing the words of the verse. Play this once a day for five days. Throughout the week, ask God to reveal one specific area, project, prayer request, desire etc. that you have given up on and ask Him to be your help to endure, persist and finish.

❑ **Mission Complete- Day 1** - Find and play the song listed above.

❑ **Mission Complete- Day 2**- Worship and praise God during the song.

❑ **Mission Complete- Day 3**- Worship and praise God during the song.

❑ **Mission Complete- Day 4**- Complete the prayer mission above while worshipping.

❑ **Mission Complete- Day 5**- Complete the prayer mission above while worshipping.

❑ **All Missions Completion Date:**

_____

❑ **Mission Notes:**

_____

_____

_____

_____

_____

_____

_____

_____

Your journal: Record your thoughts for the week. Any victories or defeat?

_____

_____

_____

_____

_____

_____

_____

_____

_____

GROUP SHARE
After Week 8

_____

_____

_____

_____

_____

_____

_____

_____

_____

_____

_____

_____

_____

_____

_____

_____

_____

_____

LET'S REVIEW.

Review is a formal assessment with the possibility or intention of instituting **change** if necessary.
(Google definition)

WEEK 9
LET'S REVIEW

Congratulations!

You made it through the first eight weeks of **Mission ME!** I hope you feel good about what you've done thus far. As I mentioned in the beginning of our journey, it won't be easy. I understand that Satan has come against some of you throughout the first eight weeks. Some of you have probably experienced life's issues. Others have experienced subtle distractions. Perhaps some of you have gone through medical issues throughout your journey or family concerns.

Regardless of what happened, please know that what you have done so far is not in vain. One of my favorite scriptures is Colossians 3:23, which states whatever you do; work at it as of working for the Lord and not unto man because you know you will receive your reward from the Lord. Of course, we are not completing the mission (solely) for the purpose of a reward. We are completing the missions for the purpose of growing closer to our Lord and Savior Jesus Christ. Please know that He sees your effort, whether great or small. And He's always right by your side waiting patiently for you because He loves you dearly.
It's never too late to start over.

Let's review:

What was the theme for week 1? *(Hint: The themes are at the top of each new week number.)*

_____

_____

_____

_____

_____

What was the theme for week 2?

_____

_____

_____

_____

What was the theme for week 3?

_____

_____

_____

_____

What was the theme for week 4?

_____

_____

_____

_____

What was the theme for week 5?

_____

_____

_____

_____

_____

What was the theme for week 6?

_____

_____

_____

What was the theme for week 7?

_____

_____

_____

What was the theme for week 8?

_____

_____

_____

Based on the first eight weeks, which week was most impactful to you?

_____

Why?

_____

_____

_____

_____

_____

Based on the first eight weeks, which week was the most challenging to do?

_____

Why?

_____

_____

_____

_____

_____

_____

_____

After the first eight weeks, share what you are doing differently in your personal relationship with Christ? If you haven't changed much, what can you do differently for the next four weeks in class? (Feel free to go back through the previous missions.)

GROUP SHARE
After Week 9

WEEK 10

ARE YOU LOVING PEOPLE...
EVEN IF YOU DON'T LIKE THEM?

*If it is possible, as far as it depends on you, live at peace with
everyone.*
Romans 12:18

What do you think about this week's title? Perhaps you
laughed and thought of a person (or group of people) that you
sort of don't like. Let's be honest: unless you're Jesus
himself, its hard going through life loving everyone.
Consider the current political climate. It's toxic. The
tribalization of Americans has caused a sad divide in our
great country. So much so, that it's hard to turn on the
television or social media without witnessing name calling,
finger pointing and nasty innuendos.
As Christians, aren't we *supposed* to love everyone and pray
for them?

Sure.

However, in reality, it doesn't always happen. We're human.

Flawed.

Corrupt.

But Jesus...

The Bible does not say we **must** like everyone. However, we
are admonished to live in peace with all men. In fact,
Romans 12:18 states, If it is possible, as far as it depends on
you, live at peace with everyone. Ephesians 4:32 reminds us
to be kind and compassionate to one another, forgiving each
other, just as Christ God forgave you.

When I think about the number of mistakes I've made and my habitual sin tendencies in light of God's unending, unyielding mercy, how can I hold ought against someone else? How could I ever hold a grudge against someone, when God so freely lavished His love and grace upon me? He set the ultimate example of love when He forgave us. How can we not follow His example?

Your scripture: Please write Psalm 63:8 in the space below:

Your scripture: Is there a person (or group) in your life (or in the world) that you have private ought against? If so, write it in the space below.

Read Psalm 66:18. How does this scripture connect your prayers and your feelings toward others?

_____

_____

_____

_____

_____

_____

_____

_____

_____

_____

_____

_____

Your Mission:

Be honest and **not** religious. Spend time thinking about the previous question regarding a person (or group of people) that you have ill-will towards. Bring this to the Lord for five days and ask Him to forgive you for not forgiving others and commit that person to the Lord. Think deeply and even globally if you have to. Is that person close or nearby? Is the person well-known or sitting across the kitchen table from you? Invite God into your heart and ask Him to give you a heart to love them.

❑ **Mission Complete- Day 1-** Identify the person/group. Pray for seven minutes.

❑ **Mission Complete- Day 2-** Pray **about** the person/group for seven minutes.

❑ **Mission Complete- Day 3-** Pray **about** the person/group for seven minutes.

❑ **Mission Complete- Day 4-** Pray **for** the person/group for seven minutes.

❑ **Mission Complete- Day 5-** Pray **for** the person/group for seven minutes.

❑ **All Missions Completion Date:**

_____

Mission Notes:

_____

_____

_____

_____

_____

_____

_____

_____

_____

Your journal: Record your thoughts for the week. Any victories or defeat?

_____

_____

_____

_____

_____

_____

_____

_____

_____

_____

_____

Philippians 4:13
(The Living Bible)

For I can do everything God asks me to with the help of Christ
who gives me the strength and power.

GROUP SHARE
After Week 10

WEEK 11
ARE YOU UNDER PRESSURE?

Cast your cares on the Lord and he will sustain you; he will never let the righteous be shaken.
Psalm 55:22

I have a trick question for you.

Why do we, as women, take on so much responsibility? Why do we often create pressurized situations in our lives? Why do we overload our "to do" list and pack out our schedules? Trust me: the questions I present are therapeutic in nature. While facilitating a recent Bible study, the topic of pressure was introduced. When I mentioned this topic, there was a loud and collective moan from the ladies. Unfortunately, we went through the week discussing it, but never getting to the root of why we take on so much. Perhaps we feel like life can't go on without us? Maybe, we think the world needs us, and so we must put on our superwoman cape every day?

Perhaps we are afraid that our husbands and families won't do things *exactly* the way we want things done?

Are we secret agent control freaks? I don't have the answer, but I know Who has the answer. Recently I turned down $2,000 a month in contracts for the sake of my sanity. Honestly, my family and I needed the additional income. However, I decided I wanted my peace more than the money. That's when I received the revelation for this chapter.

When we put ourselves in pressurized situations, we are inviting the enemy in to have a field day with our minds, hearts, and emotions. However, when we reject the notion of overloading our lives, we invite a spirit of peace in. Consider peace as the Drano that unclogs everything in your sink. If you're living a cluttered and stressful life, then I encourage you to make the change today. God will help you.

Your scripture: Please write Psalm 63:8 (again) in the space below:

_____

_____

_____

_____

_____

_____

_____

_____

_____

_____

_____

_____

Your scripture: In the NIV Bible, the Psalmist uses the word "clinging." Look up the definition of cling and write what it means on the lines below.

_____

_____

_____

_____

_____

_____

_____

_____

Are you "clinging" to God? If not, what do you think you're clinging to for help?

_____

_____

_____

_____

_____

_____

_____

Your Mission:

Look at your schedule for the week. Use the chart below to prayerfully streamline your life. Consider places you go or things you do and place them in one of three categories, such as "go to work" (MUST HAVE), "spa day" (MIGHT NEED) and "social media daily" (DOESN'T MATTER).

MUST HAVE	MIGHT NEED	DOESN'T MATTER

MUST HAVE	MIGHT NEED	DOESN'T MATTER

❏ **Mission Complete- Day 1 -** Start your chart/ Pray about it for seven minutes
❏ **Mission Complete- Day 2-** Complete your chart. Pray about it for seven minutes
❏ **Mission Complete- Day 3-** Pray about your schedule for seven minutes.
❏ **Mission Complete- Day 4-** Pray about your priorities for seven minutes.
❏ **Mission Complete- Day 5-** Pray for peace in your schedule for seven minutes.

❏ **All Missions Completion Date:**

_____

Mission Notes:

_____

_____

_____

_____

_____

_____

_____

_____

_____

Your journal: Record your thoughts for the week. Any victories or defeat?

GROUP SHARE
After Week 11

WEEK 12

_____

_____

_____

Write your own theme for the week in the line above.

And I am sure of this, that he who began a good work in you will bring it to completion at the day of Jesus Christ.
Philippians 1:6 ESV

You made it! Can you believe it? You made it to week 12 and I am proud of you.

We began this journey by acknowledging our sheer thirst for God and we'll end it with a commitment to clinging to Him. In your private time this week, you will answer a familiar question or two. Also, this final week is all about getting the Word of God that we have studied down in your heart. Romans 12:2 says we will be transformed by the renewal of our minds. The only way we can renew our minds is by getting the Word of God inside of us. Therefore, your assignment this week is to hand write Psalm 63:1-8 in the spaces below.

Your Mission is to spend the entire week reading, meditating, and attempting to memorize this entire passage. Don't worry: if you can't memorize all of it. Simply choose the verses that mean the most to you and commit them to memory in your prayer time.

Please write Psalm 63:1-8 the space below:

On a scale of 1-5 (1 being poor and 5 being outstanding), how would you rate your current spiritual temperature? (**NOTE**: *Spiritual temperature is a phrase to describe how close you sense God in your everyday life. Does He seem close and intimate or does He seem distant?*)

_____

Why?

_____

_____

_____

_____

_____

_____

_____

_____

_____

_____

_____

_____

_____

On a scale of 1-5, how would you rate your desire to grow closer to Jesus Christ?

Why?

_____

_____

_____

_____

_____

_____

_____

_____

_____

_____

_____

_____

_____

_____

_____

_____

GROUP SHARE
After Week 12

Philippians 1:6

...being confident of this, that he who began a good work in you will carry it on to completion until the day of Christ Jesus.

MISSION ACCOMPLISHED

Made in the USA
Coppell, TX
26 July 2021